THE
BIG BOOK
OF KIDS'
JOKES

Kay Barnham and Sean Connolly

ARCTURUS

ARCTURUS

ISBN 978-1-78404-966-9
CH004692NT
Supplier 29, Date 0715, Print run 4209

Written by Sean Connolly and Kay Barnham
Edited by Joe Harris
Illustrations by Adam Clay and Dynamo Design
This edition produced by Lucy Doncaster

Manufactured in China

2 4 6 8 10 9 7 5 3 1

CONTENTS

Never mind a quiet snigger, it's time to laugh out loud!
You'll struggle to contain your roaring outbursts with the
jokes in this awesome collection!

If you like to laugh, then you'll love this book of themed gags!
We've included everything from classics to one-liners, silly shaggy
dog stories to the best spoof films, song and book titles you've
never heard of, plus many, many more.

So open up this giggle-filled treasure chest and make your friends and
family smile with over 1,000 eye-wateringly funny jokes!

Why are dogs such bad dancers?
They have two left feet.

What's worse than raining cats and dogs?
Hailing taxis.

What happened to the cat that swallowed a ball of wool?
She had mittens.

How can you keep a wet dog from smelling?
Hold its nose.

Have you put some more water in the goldfish bowl?
No. It still hasn't drunk the water I put in when I first bought it!

Hey, you can't fish here, this is a private lake!
I'm not fishing, I'm teaching my pet worm to swim!

How do fleas get from one animal to another?
They itch hike!

What's the special offer at the pet store this week?
Buy one cat, get one flea!

What do you call a multi-level pigpen?
A styscraper.

Why did the dog wear
gloves?
Because it was a boxer.

ANIMAL ANTICS

My dog's a blacksmith.
How can you tell?
When I tell him off, he makes a bolt for the door.

Why did it take the Dalmatian so long to choose a vacation?
He was looking for just the right spot.

Why was the cat scared of the tree?
Because of its bark.

What animal wears a long coat in the winter and pants in the summer?
A dog!

What is a good pet for small children?
A rattlesnake!

What type of dog can tell the time?
A watchdog.

How do you spell mousetrap using only three letters?
C A T!

Which pets are the noisiest?
Trumpets!

What did the dog say when it sat on some sharp stones?
Ruff!

Classified ad in local paper:
"Dog free to good home. Eats anything. Loves children!"

How do you stop a dog from barking in the back seat of a car?
Put it in the front seat.

What are dog cookies made from?
Collie-flour!

Why did the dog limp into the Wild West saloon?
He came to find the cowboy who shot his paw!

I think I'm turning into a young cat.
You must be kitten me!

What do you call a cat that chases outlaws?
A posse cat!

What do you get if you cross an insect and a rabbit?
Bugs Bunny.

Did you hear about the well-behaved cat?
It was purrfect.

One boy says to another boy, "My pet's called Tiny."
"Why?" asks his friend.
"Because he's my newt."

Knock, knock!
Who's there?
Alf.
Alf who?
Alf feed the cat while you're abroad!

What do cats drink in the desert?
Evaporated milk.

What do you call a column topped with a statue of
a famous cat?
A caterpillar!

What do you call a cat with eight legs?
An octopus.

What do you call a woman with a cat on her head?
Kitty.

What did the dog say when his owner stopped him from chewing the newspaper?
"You took the words out of my mouth!"

What do you get if you drop birdseed in your shoes?
Pigeon toes.

What did the clean dog say to the dirty dog?
Long time no flea!

My dog is a real problem. He chases anything and everything on a bike. I don't know what to do.
Just take his bike away!

Which cats are great at bowling?
Alley cats.

What sort of dog is good at looking after children?
A baby setter.

Doctor, I think I'm a cat!
How long have you felt like this?
Since I was a kitten!

What do you get if a cat sits on a beach at Christmas?
Sandy claws!

First cat: Where do fleas go in the winter?
Second cat: Search me!

What happened to the Scottish cat who ran into the road without looking?
It was kilt!

How do you find a lost dog?
Make a sound like a bone!

Teacher: Can you define "dogmatic?"
Pupil: Is it a robot pet?

Did you hear about the cat who sucked a lemon?
He was a sourpuss.

What sport do horses like best?
Stable tennis.

What's the difference between a well-dressed gentleman and an exhausted dog?
One wears an expensive suit and the other just pants.

Doctor, I feel as sick as a dog.
I'll make an appointment for you to see a vet!

Mother: Did you put the cat out?
Kid: I didn't need to. It wasn't on fire!

What do you use to clean a cat's hair?
A catacomb.

What do you give a sick parakeet?
Tweetment!

Why was the pig covered in ink?
Because it lived in a pen.

Why do pigs make terrible drivers?
They're all road hogs.

How do you make a cat happy?
Send it to the Canary Islands!

What do you call the place where cats and dogs go to get new tails?
A retailer!

What do you call a dog who is always rushing around?
A dash-hound!

Where do you buy baby birds?
At the chickout.

What do you get if you
leave a parrot cage
open?
A polygon.

What do you get if you
cross a honeydew and
a sheepdog?
A melon collie.

Doctor, I think I'm a dog.
Well, take a seat and I'll have a look at you.
I can't, I'm not allowed on the furniture!

Did you hear about the boy who spilled spot remover
on his dog?
The dog vanished.

Why did the chicken sit on a cleaver?
She wanted to hatchet.

What did the traffic officer put on the car outside the dog kennel?
A barking ticket.

What's a dog's fave hobby?
Collecting fleas.

What does your pet snake become if he gets a government job?
A civil serpent!

Why did the cat say "woof?"
It was learning a foreign language.

What do you get when you cross a parrot and a cat?
A carrot

Where do huskies train for dogsled races?
In the mushroom.

Why did the dogs jump in the lake?
To catch a catfish.

What type of pet just lies around doing nothing?
A carpet.

What kind of dog chases anything red?
A Bulldog.

Which dog wears a white coat
and looks through microscopes?
A lab!

What do you call a prisoner's
parakeet?
A jail bird!

Why did the cat pounce on the computer?
Because he saw a mouse.

What's happening when you hear "Meow, splat! Woof, splat!"
It's raining cats and dogs.

What has more lives than a cat?
A frog. It croaks every night.

Did you hear about the cat who drank three saucers of water in one go?
She wanted to set a new lap record!

Doctor, I feel like a dog!
Sit!

Why do dogs wag their tails?
Because no one else will do it for them.

**What's red
and green and
jumps out of planes?**
A parrot-trooper!

Why did the Dalmatian go to the eye doctor?
He was seeing spots.

What did Shakespeare's cat say?
"Tabby or not tabby..."

Why do dogs run in circles?
Because it's hard to run in squares.

What do you get when you cross a dog with a sheep?
A sheep that can round itself up.

What did the cowboy say when the bear ate his hunting hound?
Doggone!

What do parakeets wear to the beach?
Beakinis.

What happens when cats fight?
They hiss and make up.

What do you call rabbits marching backward?
A receding hare-line.

What kind of bird does construction work?
A crane.

What does a cat say when it is hurt?
Mee-OW!

How did the puppy stop the DVD player?
He used paws.

What do you get when you cross a dog with an elephant?
A really nervous delivery man.

Why are dogs longer at night than during the day?
Because they are let out in the evening and taken in
in the morning.

What do you get if you mix a bird, a car, and a dog?
A flying carpet.

What kind of cat keeps the grass short?
A lawn meower.

Cat bumper sticker:
"Life is hard, then you nap."

What do you call a hamster who can pick up an elephant?
Sir!

Did you hear about the pig who walked around
the world?
He was a globetrotter.

Why is it called a "litter" of puppies?
Because they mess up the whole house.

What happened when the dog went to the flea circus?
He stole the show!

What did one flea say to the other flea?
"Should we walk or take the dog?"

FUNNY FOOD

Why did the cookie cry?
Because his mother had
been a wafer
so long.

When do truck drivers stop for a snack?
When they see a fork in the road.

What did one plate say to the other plate?
Lunch is on me.

Waiter, this food tastes funny.
Then why aren't you laughing?

Why did the rhubarb go out with a prune?
Because he couldn't find a date.

FUNNY FOOD

This coffee is disgusting, it tastes like mud.
I'm not surprised, it was ground a few minutes ago!

Why did the chef serve frozen steak?
He wanted it to melt in the mouth.

What do you get if you cross a comedian and an orange?
Peels of laughter.

What do you call an airplane passenger covered in salt and pepper?
A seasoned sightseer.

What did the speedy tomato say to the slow tomato?
Ketchup!

FUNNY FOOD

What happened at the cannibals' wedding?
They toasted the bride and groom.

Waiter, waiter, there's a button in my lettuce.
Ah! That will be from the salad dressing, sir!

Why did the man eat yeast and furniture polish for breakfast?
He wanted to rise and shine.

Knock knock.
Who's there?
Arthur.
Arthur who?
Arthur any cookies left?

How do you make a fruit punch?
Give it boxing lessons.

FUNNY FOOD

Why did the girl stare at the orange juice carton?
Because it said "concentrate" on the label.

Why was the chef so relaxed?
He had plenty of thyme on his hands!

What's yellow and dangerous?
Shark-infested custard.

Waiter, waiter, there's a fly in my soup!
Sorry, madam, I didn't know you were vegetarian!

Did you hear about the turkey who tried to escape the roasting pan?
He was foiled.

FUNNY FOOD

What are apricots?
Where baby monkeys
sleep!

How do you know
when a cannibal feels
like eating you?
He keeps buttering
you up!

What did the fat man
say when he sat down
at the dinner table?
"Just think, all this food is going to waist!"

How do you make golden soup?
Put 14 carrots in it!

What do you get if you divide the circumference of a
pumpkin by its diameter?
Pumpkin pi.

A pizza walks into a bar and asks for a burger.
"I'm sorry," says the barman.
"We don't serve food."

Chef: I didn't use a recipe for this casserole, I made it up out of my own head!
Customer: I thought it tasted of sawdust!

If I cut a potato in two, I have two halves. If I cut a potato in four, I have four quarters. What do I have if I cut a potato in 16?
French fries!

Why did the bakers work late?
Because they kneaded the dough!

How much did the pirate pay for his corn?
A buck an ear.

FUNNY FOOD

Waiter, can I have my lunch on the patio?
Certainly, sir, but most people find a plate more sensible!

Why should you never tell secrets in a corn field?
Because you would be surrounded by ears!

What farm animal can you spread on toast?
A baby goat, it's a little butter!

What's the most expensive item on the menu at a Chinese restaurant?
Fortune cookies.

Mmmmm! This cake is lovely and warm!
It should be; the cat's been sitting on it all afternoon!

What do computer operators eat for a snack?
Chips!

How do they eat their chips?
One byte at a time.

Which snack is wicked and lives in the desert?
The sand witch!

How do you keep flies out of your kitchen?
Move the pile of rotting vegetables into the living room!

What starts and ends with "t," and is also full of "t?"
A teapot.

What kind of bird is at every meal?
A swallow.

FUNNY FOOD

Why did the vampire always carry a bottle of tomato ketchup?
He was a vegetarian!

What is the one thing that stays hot in the refrigerator?
Mustard!

What did the chewing gum say to the shoe?
I'm stuck on you.

Why did the tomato blush?
Because he saw the salad dressing.

Knock knock.
Who's there?
Phil.
Phil who?
Phil this cup with sugar, would you, I've run out!

FUNNY FOOD

Why do the French like eating snails?
Because they don't like fast food!

Why is cutting a slice of gingerbread the easiest job in the world?
It's a piece of cake.

What is the best time to pick apples?
When the farmer is away!

Customer: Why is there a dead fly in my soup?
Waiter: Well, you surely don't expect to get a live one at these prices!

What did one snowman say to the other snowman?
Smells like carrots.

FUNNY FOOD

Why did the man send his alphabet soup back?
Because he couldn't find words to describe it!

Did you hear about the silly farmer who took his cows to
the North Pole, thinking he would get ice cream?

Waiter, there's half a dead cockroach in my food!
You'll have to pay for the half you've eaten, sir!

How do you eat your turkey?
I just gobble it down!

Did you hear about the eggs who kept playing tricks
on people?
They were practical yolkers.

FUNNY FOOD

Why do bees have icky,
sticky hair?
They use honeycombs.

Waiter, this crab only has
one claw!
Sorry, sir, it must have been
in a fight!
In that case, take it away and
bring me the winner.

Doctor, I think I've just swallowed a chicken bone!
Are you choking?
No, I'm serious!

What do you call a lazy baker?
A loafer!

Waiter, this muffin tastes awful!
Sir, I can assure you that our chef has been making
muffins since he was a child!
That may be true, but can I have one of his fresher
ones please?

FUNNY FOOD

Why did the lemon refuse to fight the orange?
Because it was yellow!

There's a stick insect in my salad; fetch me the branch
manager at once!

Where is the best place to keep a pie?
Your tummy!

What type of lettuce did they serve on the Titanic?
Iceberg.

FUNNY FOOD

Did you hear about the paranoid potatoes?
They kept their eyes peeled for danger.

Why do basketball players love cookies?
They can dunk them.

Why are seagulls called seagulls?
Because if they flew over bays, they would be bagels.

What did the carrot stick say to the potato chip?
"Want to go for a dip?"

What sort of dog has no tail?
A hot dog!

What do refuse collectors eat?
Junk food.

Teacher: Sally, give me a sentence with the word "aroma" in it.
Sally: My uncle Fred is always on the go; he's aroma!

Teacher: Philip, why do you have a lunchbox in each hand?
Philip: It's important to have a balanced diet, Mr. Harrison!

What do you get if you mix birdseed with your breakfast cereal?
Shredded tweet.

What is worse than finding a worm in your apple?
Finding half a worm in your apple!

What snack food
do cannibals
love best?
Pizza with
everyone
on it.

What did
the golfer
eat for lunch?
A sand wedge.

Why are clocks greedy?
They always have seconds.

Why couldn't Batman go fishing?
Because Robin had eaten all the worms.

Did you hear about the strawberry who attended
charm school?
He became a real smoothie.

Which part of Swiss cheese is the least fattening?
The holes!

What do you call a pig who does karate?
A pork chop.

Why did the potato cry?
Its peelings were hurt.

How do you make a stiff drink?
Put cement in your cup.

Did you hear about Professor Cole, the scientist who discovered the perfect ratio for mixing cabbage, carrot, onion, and mayonnaise?
He called it Cole's Law.

Why did the girl disappear into the bowl of cereal?
A strong currant pulled her under.

Knock knock.
Who's there?
Police.
Police who?
Police can I have a chocolate milkshake?

What kind of nut always has a cold?
A cashew!

What do you call a fake noodle?
An impasta.

Johnny! How many more times do I have to tell you to keep away from the cookie jar?
No more times; it's empty!

What do you get if you cross a chicken with a cement mixer?
A bricklayer.

FUNNY FOOD

Does Dracula's chef ever cook roast beef?
Yes, but very rarely.

What dessert do chickens love best?
Layer cake!

Knock knock.
Who's there?
Anita.
Anita who?
Anita nother hot dog, I'm starving!

How do you fix a broken
pizza?
With tomato paste!

Why did the man
wear a
banana skin
on each
foot?
He wanted a
pair of slippers.

MONSTER FUN

MONSTER FUN

Where do ghosts swim?
In the Dead Sea.

What did the vampire doctor say?
Necks please!

Did you hear about the banshee who wanted to be an actress?
She did a scream test.

What does a dragon call a knight?
Canned food!

What do you get if you cross a vampire with a circus entertainer ?
Someone who goes straight for the juggler!

What do you get if you cross a vampire with a mummy?
Something you wouldn't want to unwrap!

What do ghosts eat for dinner?
Ghoulash!

How do ghosts begin business letters?
"Tomb it may concern..."

Why didn't the skeleton fight the monster?
He didn't have the guts!

What has a pointy hat, a broomstick, and a blue face?
A witch holding her breath.

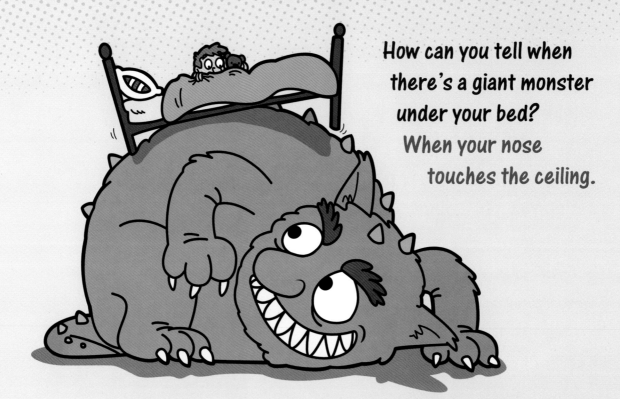

How can you tell when there's a giant monster under your bed? When your nose touches the ceiling.

What happened to the vampire with bad breath?
His dentist told him to gargoyle twice a day!

What do vampires do at eleven o'clock every night?
They have a coffin break.

What was written on the robot's gravestone?
Rust in pieces!

How does Frankenstein's monster sit in a chair?
Bolt upright!

How do you know that smoking is harmful to your health?
Well, look what happened to all the dragons!

Should monsters eat people on an empty stomach?
No, they should eat them on a plate!

What is a monster's fave party game?
Swallow the leader!

Why don't skeletons sing church music?
They have no organs.

What goes "WOO-HA-HA" THUMP?
Frankenstein's monster laughing his head off.

What job does Dracula have with the Transylvanian baseball team?
He looks after the bats!

Why do ghosts never feel guilty?
They have a clear conscience!

First friend: Did you know that you can get fur from a vampire?
Second friend: Really? What kind of fur?
First friend: As fur away as possible!

Why do vampires dislike computers?
They hate anything new-fang-led!

Why did the car stop when it saw the monster truck?
It had a nervous breakdown.

Why was young Dr. Frankenstein so popular?
Because he was great at making new friends!

How did you know I was a ghost?
Oh, I can see right through you!

How did the ghostly teacher make sure his pupils had learned what he had written on the board?
He went through it again!

Why did the monster buy a hatchet?
Because he wanted to get a-head in life!

How do vampires get clean?
In a blood bath!

MONSTER FUN

Why wasn't the werewolf astronaut allowed to land
his spaceship?
Because the moon was full!

Who do vampires invite to their birthday parties?
Anybody they can dig up!

Why did Dracula advertise for a housekeeper?
He wanted some new blood in the house!

Who is the world's scariest superhero?
Vampire bat-man!

What sort of telescope lets you see ghosts?
A horrorscope!

What do you call a lazy skeleton?
Bone idle!

What did Frankenstein do when the monster's head kept falling off?
He made a bolt for it!

Why do monsters like to stand in a ring?
They love being part of a vicious circle!

Where do werewolves live?
In warehouses.

Why doesn't Dracula have any friends?
Because he's a pain in the neck!

What does Dracula drink?
"De-coffin-ated" coffee!

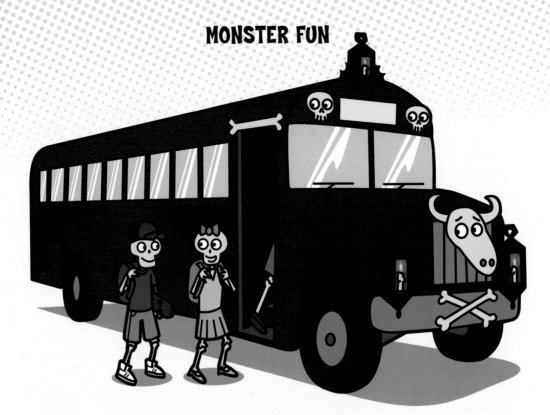

"Hurry up," said the father skeleton to his son, "or you'll be late for the skull bus!"

What do you call a kind, helpful monster who likes flowers and butterflies?
A failure!

What did the old vampire say when he broke his teeth?
Fangs for the memory...

What does it say on the mummy's garage entrance?
Toot, and come in!

Who was the winner of the headless horse race?
No one. They all finished neck and neck!

Why are you throwing garlic out of the window?
To keep vampires away.
But there aren't any vampires here.
See, it works!

Why did the giant robot feel sick after eating a train?
He caught a commuter virus!

If having hairy palms is the first sign of turning into a monster, what is the second?
Looking for them!

Why did Godzilla stop eating buildings?
He got atomic ache!

MONSTER FUN

What do ghosts do if they are afraid?
Hide under a sheet!

Why did the monster have twins in his lunchbox?
In case he felt like seconds!

Why didn't the vampire laugh at the joke about the wooden stake?
He didn't get the point!

Why did the werewolf swallow a bag full of coins?
Because he thought the change would do him good!

Why do zombies always look so tired?
They are dead on their feet!

What is the first thing a monster eats when he goes to a restaurant?
The waiter!

What do monsters call a crowded swimming pool?
Soup!

Why did the robot need a manicure?
He had rusty nails!

Why didn't the phantom win the lottery?
He didn't have a ghost of a chance!

Why do football teams have to try extra hard when they play against zombies?
Because they face stiff competition!

MONSTER FUN

What did the young ghost call his mother and father?
His trans-parents!

Why do little monsters not mind being eaten by ghosts?
Because they know they will always be in good spirits!

Why are there more ghost dogs than ghost cats?
Because every cat has nine lives!

Why do monster parents tell their children to eat cabbage?
Because they want them to have a healthy green complexion!

MONSTER FUN

Which monster is the most untidy?
The Loch Mess Monster!

Why did the cyclops school close down?
Because they only had one pupil!

Why are vampires close to their families?
Because blood is thicker than water!

Why do other monsters find mummies vain?
They're so wrapped up in themselves.

Why do vampires never invite trolls to their
dinner parties?
They can't stand all that goblin!

MONSTER FUN

What do you call a ghostly chicken?
A poultry-geist.

Why did the zombie go to the doctor?
He wanted something to help stop his coffin.

What do you call a child vampire?
A pain in the knee!

Who do vampires invite to their weddings?
All their blood relatives!

How does a skeleton know when it's going to rain?
He just gets a feeling in his bones!

Why don't ghosts do aerobics?
Because they don't want to be exorcised!

Why are owls so brave at night?
Because they don't give a hoot for ghosts, monsters, or vampires!

How do vampires show affection for each other?
They bat their eyelids!

What is the first thing you should put into a haunted house?
Someone else!

Why did Goldilocks go to Egypt?
She wanted to see the mummy bear!

What did the werewolf say to the skeleton?
It's been so nice getting to gnaw you!

Why did the ghost go to the bicycle shop?
He needed some new spooks for his front wheel!

What do you get if you cross the Abominable Snowman with Count Dracula?
Severe frostbite!

What did the witch call her baby daughter?
Wanda!

What do you need to pick up a giant's silverware?
A forklift.

What do you call a male vampire in women's clothing?
Drag-cula!

How do you make a skeleton laugh?
Just tickle his funny bone.

Knock knock!
Who's there?
Russia!
Russia who?
Russia way, a monster's coming!

Why was the genie in the lamp angry?
Someone rubbed him up the wrong way!

MONSTER FUN

What do you get if you cross a warlock with a laptop?
A computer wizard!

What do skeletons say before eating?
Bone appetit!

What do you call the jewels that ghosts wear?
Tombstones!

What do dinosaurs rest their teacups on?
Tyrannosaucers.

MONSTER FUN

How do you help Frankenstein's monster?
Give him a hand when he needs it!

How do witch children listen to stories?
Spellbound!

How can you tell
when a robot
is angry?
It flips its lid!

What sort of drink do
monsters slurp?
Lemon and slime.

Book spotted in the school library:
The Haunted House by Hugo First.

What do you call a hairy monster who's lost
his way home?
A where-am-I wolf.

What happens when a witch catches the flu?
Everyone gets a cold spell!

Why do vampires have a steady nerve?
They are as ghoul as cucumbers!

Why don't vampires write their own books?
They prefer to use ghost writers!

Where do monsters like to go on vacation?
Death Valley!

SPACE SILLINESS

Where do you find black holes?
In black socks.

What makes you think my son could be an astronaut?
He has nothing but space between his ears!

Did you hear about the woman who went in for plastic surgery, and came out looking like a Martian?
She told the surgeon she wanted to look like a million dollars, so he made her face all green and crinkly!

Which weighs the most, a full moon or a half moon?
A half moon, because a full moon is much lighter!

How do you get a baby astronaut to sleep?
Rocket.

Knock knock.
Who's there?
Jupiter.
Jupiter who?
Jupiter spaceship
on my lawn?

Teacher: William,
how fast does light
travel?
William: I don't know,
it's already arrived by
the time I wake up!

Which is the most stylish planet?
Saturn. It has a lot of rings.

When can you be sure that the moon won't eat you?
When it's a full moon.

What crazy bug lives on the moon?
The lunar tick.

An astronaut and a chimp were fired off into space.
The chimp opened its sealed orders, read them, and
immediately started programming the flight computer.
The astronaut opened his sealed orders and found only
one instruction:
"Feed the chimp!"

How do aliens go fishing?
With Earth-worms!

What lies at the heart of gravity?
The letter V.

Why do little green men have nice, warm homes?
Because they live in little greenhouses!

Why didn't the astronaut get burned when he
landed on the sun?
He went there at night!

Why are parties on the moon always so dull?
There's no atmosphere.

Why do astronomers always bang their heads?
It helps them to see stars!

Book spotted in the school library:
Is There Life on Mars? by Howard I. No.

Three badly made robots were playing cards.
The first one threw his hand in.
The second one rolled his eyes.
The third one laughed his head
off.

SPACE SiLLiNESS

Why don't astronauts keep their jobs for long?
Because after their training they're always fired.

What did one rocket say to the other?
I wish I could quit smoking!

Some meteorites collide with planets. What do you call
meteorites that miss?
Meteowrongs.

Why did the alien turn the restaurant staff
upside down?
Someone told him that you had to tip the waiter!

What did one asteroid say to the other asteroid?
"Pleased to meteor."

What do aliens cook their
breakfasts on?
Unidentified frying objects.

What do young astronauts sit on
during takeoff?
Booster seats.

How does the solar
system hold up
its clothes?
With an
asteroid belt.

What did the boy star
say to the girl star?
Do you want to glow out with me?

Why did the alien build a spaceship from feathers?
He wanted to travel light years!

What type of snack does an alien love best?
A Martian-mallow.

SPACE SILLINESS

Why do astronauts have to prepare a meal before blastoff?
They get hungry at launch time.

Why do astronauts make good American football players?
They know how to make a great touchdown!

Why was the thirsty astronaut loitering near the computer keyboard?
He was looking for the space bar.

Big alien: If this planet is Mars, what's that one over there?
Little alien: Is it Pa's?

SPACE SILLINESS

Did you know that they have found life on another planet?
Really?
Yes, there are fleas on Pluto!

What holds the moon up?
Moon beams.

Why did the Sun go to school?
To get brighter.

Why are grandma's teeth
like stars?
Because they come out at night.

Where do you leave your spaceship
when you visit another planet?
At a parking meteor!

SPACE SILLINESS

Why do cats hate flying saucers?
Because they can't reach the milk!

What was the first animal in space?
The cow that jumped over the moon.

Which actor won the Martian Oscars?
Kevin Outer-Spacey!

Why do astronauts never diet?
No one needs to lose weight in space, because
everything is weightless!

**Why did the spaceship land
outside my bedroom?**
You must have left
the landing light on!

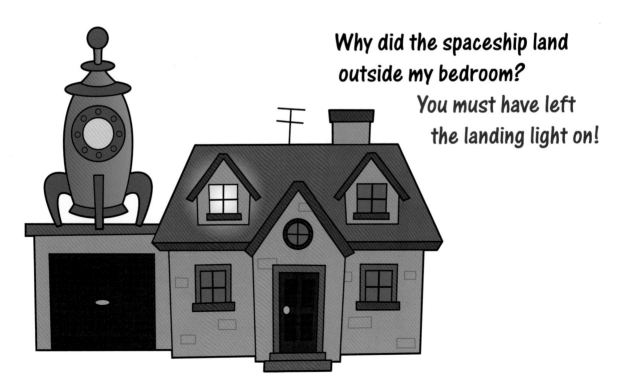

What's an
alien's
preferred
drink?
Gravi-tea.

What did Saturn
say when Jupiter
asked if he could call
him?
"Don't call me. I'll give
you a ring."

What's normal eyesight for a Martian?
20-20-20!

What should you do if you see a spaceman?
Park your car in it, man!

I don't know what to buy my pal, the space alien, for
his birthday.
How about five-and-a-half pairs of slippers?

What does an alien gardener do with his hedges?
Eclipse them every spring!

Why did the alien launch a clock into space?
He wanted to see time fly.

How did the alien tie his shoelaces?
With an astro-knot.

Why don't aliens celebrate each other's birthdays?
They don't like to give away their presents.

What's faster than the speed of light?
The speed of dark!

Which cartoon character is popular with robots?
Tin-tin!

When is a window like a star?
When it's a skylight.

If an athlete gets athlete's foot, what does an
astronaut get?
Missile toe!

What is covered in
wool and comes
from outer space?
A ewe-F-O.

How did the aliens hurt the farmer?
They landed on his corn.

What do you call an overweight alien?
An extra-cholesterol.

First astronomer: Do you think there's intelligent life out there?
Second astronomer: I doubt it. All the aliens I've met are pretty stupid!

Why did the robot go crazy?
He had a screw loose.

Why couldn't the alien's spaceship travel at the speed of light?
Because he took off in the dark!

What do you call a sick space monster?
An ailin' alien.

Spotted on the science shelf of the school library:
Fly Me to the Moon
by Tay Cough

Why did the boy become an astronaut?
Because his teacher told him he was no Earthly good.

Why are astronauts such successful people?
They always go up in the world.

Which is more useful, the sun or the moon?
The moon, because it shines at night when you want the light. The sun shines during the day, when you don't really need it!

What did the alien say to the gas pump?
"Don't you know it's rude to stick your finger in your ear
when I'm talking to you?"

I've given up on time travel.
Why?
There's no future in it.

Living on Earth may be expensive, but it does include a
free trip around the sun each year.

Why are there no Martian tourists at the Grand Canyon?
Because it looks so much like home!

SPACE SILLINESS

How do you phone the sun?
You use a sun-dial.

Mars got sent to prison after the big robbery trial.
Why? He wasn't even there!
Yes, but he helped to planet.

What is a light year?
The same as a normal year,
but with fewer calories.

What did the astronaut say to his
alien girlfriend?
"You're out of this world!"

What do astronauts wear
in bed?
Space jammies.

How do aliens stay clean?
They take meteor showers.

SPACE SILLINESS

What board game do aliens love best?
Moon-opoly!

How do astronauts serve drinks?
In sunglasses.

How do aliens keep from falling over in a spaceship?
They Klingon.

Why do astronauts find it hard to mix with other people?
They're not really down to Earth.

Why does Superman wear such big shoes?
Because of his amazing feats.

Clones are
people, two.

Have you seen the movie about
toads in space?
It's called Star Warts.

What music do astronauts love best?
Rocket and roll.

Did you hear about the resentful robot?
He had a microchip on his shoulder.

What should you do if you meet a little green man?
Come back when he's a little riper.

SPACE SILLINESS

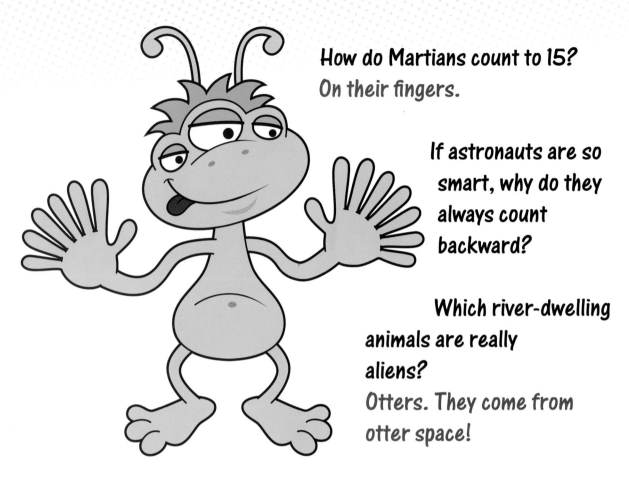

How do Martians count to 15?
On their fingers.

If astronauts are so smart, why do they always count backward?

Which river-dwelling animals are really aliens?
Otters. They come from otter space!

How many Martians does it take to screw in a light bulb?
Millions! One to hold the bulb, and the rest to turn the planet.

What did the loser in the astronomy contest receive?
The constellation prize.

What was the dentist's best subject at school?
Flossophy.

What did the number 0 say to the number 8?
"That's a cool belt."

What do you get if you cross a vampire with a teacher?
Blood tests.

Why did the teacher wear sunglasses?
Because his class was so bright.

Why did the teacher jump into the swimming pool?
He wanted to test the water.

What kind of lunches do geometry teachers enjoy?
Square meals.

Principal: You'll start with a low salary, but I'll double it in six months.
Teacher: In that case I think I would like to start in six months!

Why was the cross-eyed teacher's class rioting?
She couldn't control her pupils.

Why was the broom late for school?
It overswept.

What is a polygon?
A dead parrot.

Did you hear about the cannibal who was expelled from school?
He was buttering up the teachers.

Teacher: What language do they speak in Cuba?
Pupil: Cubic!

Why did one pencil tell the other pencil it looked old and tired?
Because it was blunt.

What's the tastiest class at school?
History. It's full of dates.

My music teacher said I have a heavenly voice!
That's not strictly true; she said your voice was like
nothing on Earth!

Teacher: You missed school yesterday, didn't you?
Pupil: Not very much!

What sum do teachers like best?
The summer.

Teacher: Why are you taking
that sponge into class?
Pupil: Because I find your
classes so absorbing!

Why was the mathematics
textbook miserable?
It had too many problems.

Why was the music teacher locked out of his classroom?
The keys were on the piano.

English teacher: Give me an example of a long sentence.
Pupil: Life imprisonment.

What did the pencil say to the protractor?
Take me to your ruler.

I sprained my ankle and had to miss gym for two weeks.
Lucky you. Our gym teacher never accepts a lame excuse for his class!

Why don't leopards bother to cheat in exams?
Because they know they will always be spotted!

Is the mathematics teacher in a good mood today?
I wouldn't count on it!

Teacher: Can you define the word "hardship?"
Silly pupil: Is it a boat made out of concrete?

My English teacher is a real peach!
You mean she's pretty?
No. I mean she has a heart of stone!

What do history teachers do before they get married?
They go out on dates!

Why is 6 afraid of 7?
Because 7 ate 9!

Parent: Why have you given my son such a bad mark? He's as intelligent as the next boy!
Teacher: Yes, but the next boy is an idiot!

Teacher: Eat up your school lunch, it's full of iron.
Pupil: That explains why it's so difficult to chew!

Teacher: How did people spend their time in the Stone Age?
Pupil: Did they listen to rock music?

Parent: Do you think my son has what it takes to become a pilot?
Teacher: Well, he certainly spends plenty of time with his head in the clouds!

What happens when music teachers are sick?
They send in a note!

History teacher: How
would you discover what
life in Ancient Egypt was
really like?
Pupil: I'd ask my mummy!

Did you hear about the
mathematics teacher whose
mistakes started to multiply?
In the end, they had to take
him away!

Why does your teacher have
her hair in a bun?
Because she has a face like
a burger!

Why do kindergarten teachers have such a positive attitude?
They know how to make the little things count.

Parent: Do you think my son will make a good Arctic explorer?
Teacher: I would think so: most of his grades are below zero!

Teacher: Can you tell me what water is?
Pupil: It's a clear liquid that turns black when I put my hands in it!

Why is that boy locked up in a cage in the corner of the classroom?
Oh, he's the teacher's pet!

I think our school must
be haunted.
Why?
Because the
teacher keeps
talking about the
school spirit!

Teacher: Who
discovered
Pluto?
Pupil: Walt Disney!

Teacher: Michael, how do we know that the Earth
is round?
Michael: I didn't say it was, Mr. Johnson!

Teacher: If you multiply 245 by 3,456 and divide the
answer by 165, then subtract 752, what will you get?
Pupil: The wrong answer!

Teacher: How good are you at picking up music?
Pupil: Well, I'm not sure if I could lift a whole piano!

Teacher: Mary, how did you find the questions in your English test?
Mary: Oh, I found the questions easily enough, it's the answers I couldn't find!

Teacher: Please don't talk while you are doing your exam.
Pupil: It's all right, Miss Brown. We're not doing the exam, just talking!

Where do vampire schoolchildren go for field trips?
Lake Eerie!

How does a teacher remove hard wax from his ears?
He works it out with a pencil!

Teacher: Why were you late this morning, Veronica?
Veronica: I squeezed the toothpaste too hard, and it took me half an hour to get it all back into the tube again!

Pupil: Can we do some work on the Iron Age today?
Teacher: Well, I'm not certain, I'm a bit rusty on that period of history!

Ten cats were at the movies. One walked out. How many were left?
None, they were all copycats!

Teacher: What was Robin Hood's mum called?
Pupil: Mother Hood.

What did you learn in school today?
Not enough. I have to go back tomorrow!

Teacher: Did you know that most accidents happen in the kitchen?
Pupil: Yes, but we still have to eat them!

Mother: Time to get up and go to school!
Son: I don't want to go! Everyone hates me and I get bullied!
Mother: But you have to go, you're the principal!

Teacher: How many seconds are there in a year?
Pupil: Twelve: January 2nd, February 2nd...

What did the music teacher need a ladder for?
Reaching the high notes!

I banged my head on the locker door this morning!
Have you seen the school nurse?
No, just stars!

Teacher: Why is your homework late, young man?
Pupil: Sorry, Miss Elliot, my dad is a slow writer!

How do archeologists get into locked tombs, young man?
Do they use a skeleton key, Mr. Edwards?

Mathematics teacher: What are net profits?
Pupil: What fishermen have left after paying the crew!

I'm not really interested in mathematics: I just go along to the lesson to make up the numbers!

What was the blackbird doing in the school library?
Looking for bookworms!

Did you hear about the gym teacher who used to run
around the classroom in order to jog pupils' memories?

Why did the school orchestra have such awful manners?
Because it didn't know how to conduct itself!

Teacher: In the future, all trains and buses will run
on time.
Pupil: Won't they run on fuel, just like now?

Teacher: I wish you'd pay a little attention!
Pupil: I'm paying as little as I can!

Young man, I hope I don't catch you cheating in the math test!
So do I, Miss Goldman!

What breed of dog do science teachers like best?
A lab!

When do 2 and 2 make more than 4?
When they make 22!

Sign outside the music department:
Violin for sale. Good price.
No strings attached!

Teacher: Why was the invention of the safety match an important change?

Pupil: It was a striking achievement!

Why did the school cafeteria hire a dentist?

To make more filling meals!

Parent: Do you think my son could work as a DJ on the radio?

Teacher: He certainly has the face for it!

Why are teachers always welcome in pool halls?

Because they always bring their own chalk!

How do you know your school bus is old?

The seats are covered in mammoth hide!

Why did the burglar break into the music department?
He was after the lute!

Why was Cinderella terrible at football?
Because her coach was a pumpkin!

Did you hear about the mathemathics teacher and the art teacher who used to go out together?
They spent their time painting by numbers!

Teacher: This homework looks as though it has been written by your father.
Pupil: Of course it does, I borrowed his pen!

Teacher: Which two words in the English language have the most letters?
Pupil: "Post Office!"

SCHOOL'S COOL

Teacher: Where were all the kings and queens of France crowned?
Pupil: On the head!

Teacher: Which age did the mummies live in?
Pupil: The Band-Age!

Where did King Arthur's men get their training?
At knight school!

What were the 16 schoolboys playing in the telephone booth?
Squash!

What sort of ring is always square?
A boxing ring!

How many librarians does it take to change a lightbulb?
Two. One to screw it in and one to say, "Shhhhhh!" at the squeaking noise.

Book seen in the school library:
The Survivors' Guide to Escaping from a Sinking Ship
by Mandy Lifeboats

What do you say to the school's best pole vaulter?
Hiya!

Geography teacher: Where is the English Channel?
Pupil: I don't know, my TV doesn't have that one!

Why did the silly pupil buy a seahorse?
Because he wanted to play water polo!

Mum: Why didn't you come straight home from school?
Daughter: Because we live around the corner!

Where do you find a giant scholar?
Around the neck of a giant's shirt.

In a family with seven children, why was the youngest late for school?
The alarm was set for six.

Which tables don't they teach you in mathematics class?
Dinner tables.

History teacher: Which renowned knight never won a single battle?
Pupil: Sir Endor!

SiLLY SAFARi

What did the blue whale say when he crashed into the bottlenose dolphin?
"I didn't do it on porpoise."

Where do reindeer run round and round in circles?
In Lapland.

What side of a porcupine is the sharpest?
The outside.

What do you call a giraffe with one leg?
Eileen.

Why did the lion
spit out the clown?
Because he tasted
funny.

What did the tiger eat
after he'd had all his
teeth pulled out?
The dentist.

What do you call a sheep
with no legs?
A cloud.

Why do giraffes
have such long
necks?
Because they
have very
smelly feet.

What do you call someone who lives with a pack
of wolves?
Wolfgang.

What does an octopus
wear in the winter?
A coat of arms.

What do you call an
elephant in a phone
booth?
Stuck.

Where do
sharks come
from?
Finland.

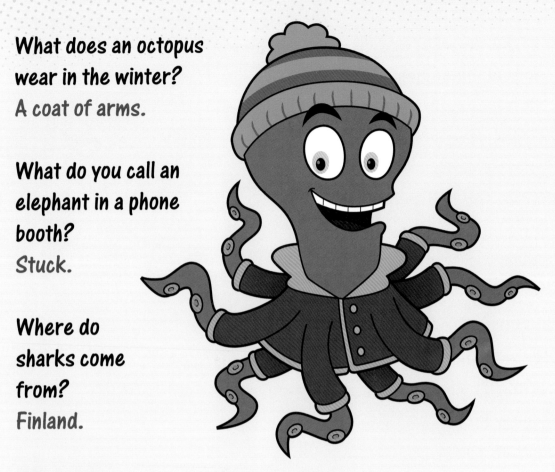

What's the
difference between a fish and a piano?
You can't tuna fish!

Why do insects hum?
Because they can never remember the words!

What's the best way to catch a fish?
Get someone to throw it at you.

What's black and white and red all over?
A sunburned penguin!

What do you get if you cross a crocodile with a camera?
A snapshot!

Where are elephants found?
They're so huge, it's quite difficult to lose them in
the first place.

Why wasn't the girl scared when a shark swam past her?
She'd been told it was a man-eater.

**What's an
elephant's
fave
game?**
Squash.

SILLY SAFARI

A police officer saw a man walking down the street with a penguin. He told the man to take the penguin to the zoo. "Good idea," the man said, and off he went.
The next day, the police officer saw the man again. He still had the penguin with him.
"I told you to take that penguin to the zoo," the police officer said.
"I did," the man replied. "He really enjoyed that, so today I'm taking him to the movies."

First leopard: Hey, is that a jogger over there?
Second leopard: Yes, great, I love fast food!

What do you get if you cross a snake with a bird?
A feather boa constrictor!

What has four legs, big ears, and a trunk?
A mouse going on vacation.

SILLY SAFARI

What did the short-sighted
porcupine say to the
cactus?
"Ah, there you
are, Dad!"

What do penguins
do in their spare time?
They chill.

Spotted in the library:
I Fell Down a Rabbit Hole by Alison Wonderland.

What do you call a dead skunk?
Ex-stinked!

Why was the mother firefly sad?
Because her children weren't very bright!

What is the best thing to do when a hippo sneezes?
Get out of the way!

SILLY SAFARI

What lives in a
forest and tells the
dullest stories
ever heard?
A wild boar!

What did the
silliest kid in
school call
his pet zebra?
"Spot!"

What would you do if a
jellyfish stung you?
I'd break every bone in its body!

What does a frog use to put up shelves?
A toad's tool!

How did the fruit bats go into Noah's Ark?
In pears!

SILLY SAFARI

Why are hyenas always falling out?
They always have a bone to pick with each other!

What are the scariest dinosaurs?
Terror dactyls!

What do you call a criminal bird?
An illegal eagle!

What sort of fish would you find in a bird cage?
A perch!

What sort of horses do monsters ride?
Night mares!

Why was the zebra put in charge of the jungle army?
Because he had the most stripes!

How do you catch a squirrel?
Climb a tree and act like a nut.

What's big, furry, and flies?
A hot-air baboon.

How do you stop moles from digging up your lawn?
Hide the shovels.

What's the difference between a crazy rabbit and a
counterfeit bank note?
One's a mad bunny and the other's bad money.

What sea creatures do you find on legal documents?
Seals.

Why should you never trust a whale with your deepest, darkest secrets?
Because they're all blubbermouths.

Where do camels keep their money?
In sand banks.

Where do tadpoles change into frogs?
In a croakroom.

What sort of animal will never oversleep?
A llama clock!

What do rhinoceroses have that no other animal has?
Baby rhinoceroses.

What do you get if you cross an angry sheep with a mad cow?
An animal that's in a baaaaaaaaaaaaaaad moooooooooooooood.

Why can't leopards hide from hunters?
Because they are always spotted!

When do kangaroos propose marriage?
In leap years!

Where do rabbits learn to fly?
In the Hare Force!

Did you hear
about the spiders
who got
married?
They had a huge
webbing.

What job did the
spider get?
Web designer!

What do you call
a worm in a fur
coat?
A caterpillar!

What do you call a bad-tempered bee?
A grumblebee.

Doctor, I think I'm a frog.
So what's the problem?
I'm sure I'm going to croak.

SILLY SAFARI

What do you get if you cross a dinosaur with a fish?
Jurassic shark!

What do you call a phone for alligators?
A croco-dial!

Did you hear about the wizard who made honey?
He was a spelling bee!

What do you call pigs who write to each other?
Pen pals!

How do elephants travel?
In jumbo jets!

SILLY SAFARI

What do camels wear when they play hide-and-seek?
Camel-flage.

What TV show do porpoises like best?
Whale of Fortune.

What do you get if you cross a sheep with a bucket of water?
A wet blanket.

What did the rabbit say when it went bald?
Hare today, gone tomorrow!

Which bird is always out of breath?
A puffin.

SILLY SAFARI

Why do sick crabs walk sideways?
Because their medicine has side-effects!

What should you do if you see a blue whale?
Try to cheer him up.

What did the celebrity squirrels sign before they got married?
A pre-nutshell agreement.

How can you tell if there's an elephant in the refrigerator?
You can't shut the door!

Why did the elephant refuse to play cards with his two friends?
Because one of them was lion and the other was a cheetah!

What do you call an owl who robs the rich and gives to the poor?
Robin Hoot!

What do toads say when they greet each other?
"Wart's new with you?"

What is a goat's preferred food?
Alpha-butt soup!

What do you get if you cross a leopard and a bunch of flowers?
A beauty spot!

Doctor, I think I'm a crocodile!
Don't worry, you'll soon snap out of it!

How do you get around on
the seabed?
By taxi-crab!

What went into
the lion's cage
at the zoo and
came out
without a
scratch?
Another lion!

Why was the
mother flea
depressed?
All her children had gone to the dogs!

How do you know if there's an elephant in your
refrigerator?
Look for footprints in the butter!

How do you get down from a camel?
You don't. You get down from a goose.

SiLLY SAFARi

How do you stop a rhinoceros from charging?
Take away its cash register.

What happened to the shark who swallowed a bunch of keys?
He got lockjaw!

Which animal was out of bounds?
The exhausted kangaroo.

What do you give a deaf fish?
A herring aid.

What do you call a hippo at the South Pole?
Lost!

SILLY SAFARI

What do you get if you cross a snake with a builder?
A boa constructor.

Where does a blackbird go for a drink?
To a crowbar.

What do porcupines say when they hug?
"Ouch!"

What do you get if you cross a fish with an elephant?
Swimming trunks.

What do you call a monkey who is king of the jungle?
Henry the Ape!

What do you call
an 85-year-old
ant?
An antique!

What do horses
wear at the
beach?
Clip clops.

Why do rabbits
have fur coats?
Because they'd
look silly in
leather jackets.

Teacher: Billy,
what is a
wombat?
Pupil: It's what you use to play "wom," Miss!

Why did the hyena do so badly at school?
He thought everything was a joke.

SILLY SAFARI

Who do fish borrow
money from?
A loan shark.

Knock knock!
Who's there?
Orang.
Orang who?
Orang the doorbell
but no one
answered, so now
I'm knocking!

What has 50 legs?
Half a centipede!

On the school field trip a crab bit my toe!
Which one?
I don't know, all crabs look the same to me!

What made the fly fly?
The spider spied her.

JOLLY JUNGLE

Why should you never trust a giraffe?
They are always telling tall stories.

What do elephants take to help them sleep?
Trunkquilizers!

What flies through the jungle singing opera?
The Parrots of Penzance.

Teacher: What do you think a pair of alligator shoes would cost?
Pupil: That would depend on the size of your alligator's feet!

Why do elephants paint their toenails red?
So they can hide in cherry trees!

JOLLY JUNGLE

What were Tarzan's last words?
"Who greased the v-i-i-i-i-i-i-i-n-e?"

Who won the giraffe race?
Nobody knows because the competitors were neck and neck.

How do you make orange crush?
Get an elephant to jump up and down in the fruit and vegetable aisle!

How do hippos commute?
By hippopotabus.

What kind of key opens a banana?
A monkey!

What sort of dancing will elephants do in your front room?
Break dancing!

Why can't I get the king of the jungle on the telephone?
Because the lion is busy!

Teacher: Have you written your essay on big cats?
Pupil: I thought it would be safer to use paper!

What do you call a lion with toothache?
Rory!

What do you call a hippo that always claims to be sick?
A hippochondriac.

Why did the firefly
keep crashing?
He wasn't very
bright.

What did King
Kong say when
he was told that
his sister had
had a baby?
"Well, I'll be a
monkey's uncle!"

What do you call a show
full of lions?
The mane event.

Why did the monkey like the banana?
Because it had appeal!

Who is in charge of the stick insects?
The branch manager!

Knock, knock!
Who's there?
Orange!
Orange who?
Orange you glad to see me?

Spotted in the jungle library:
Why Giant Snails Get Tired by Michelle Sevy

Baby snake: Dad, are we poisonous?
Dad snake: No, son, why do you ask?
Baby snake: I've just bitten my tongue!

What do you call an alligator private eye?
An investi-gator.

What do you get if you cross a tarantula with a rose?
We're not sure, but don't try smelling it!

Why don't bananas sunbathe?
Because they would peel.

What happens if you cross a hummingbird with a doorbell?
You get a humdinger.

What does the lemur do every evening?
He curls up with his best-loved tail.

What do you call a lion with no eyes?
Lon!

JOLLY JUNGLE

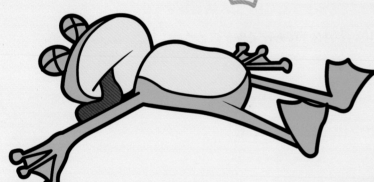

Why does a
frog have more
lives than a cat?
Because it croaks
every night.

How do you fix a broken chimp?
With a monkey wrench!

What's orange and
sounds like a parrot?
A carrot.

Is it hard to spot a leopard?
Not at all, they come that way!

What do toucans sing at Christmas?
Jungle Bells.

What advice did the parrot give to the toucan?
Talk is cheep.

What do monkeys wear when they cook?
Ape-rons.

How did the monkey get down the stairs?
It slid down the banana-ster.

What did the snake give his date when he dropped her off?
A goodnight hiss.

Why did the leopard refuse to take a bath?
Because he didn't
want to become
spotless.

What language do oranges speak?
Mandarin.

Why should you never tell a giraffe a secret?
Because you could fall off his neck as you whisper in his ear.

What did Tarzan tell his son?
"Be careful, it's a jungle out there."

What's sweet and crunchy and swings through the trees?
A meringue-utan.

What's worse than a crocodile with a toothache?
A centipede with athlete's foot.

What ice-cream does a gorilla like best?
Chocolate chimp.

Why do giraffes have small appetites?
Because a little goes a long way.

What is hairy and orange and always comes back to you?
A boomerang-utan.

What happens if you upset a cannibal?
You get into hot water.

What do you get if you cross a gorilla with a porcupine?
A seat on the bus!

Which animals were the last to leave Noah's Ark?
The elephants; they had to pack their trunks.

What do you give a gorilla that's going to throw up?
Plenty of room!

What happens if you cross an elephant and a canary?
A very messy cage.

What class do snakes like best at school?
Hisssstory.

What's the most dangerous animal in your backyard?
The clothes-lion.

What do you call an exploding ape?
A ba-BOOM!

What did the banana say to the gorilla?
Nothing, bananas can't talk!

What do you get if you cross a snake with a pig?
A boar constrictor.

What do you get when you cross an elephant with a kangaroo?
Big holes all over Australia.

Why did the leopard eat the tightrope walker?
He wanted a balanced diet.

Why do elephants never forget?
Because no one ever tells them anything.

What's the best time to buy parakeets?
When they're going cheep.

Why are anteaters so healthy?
Because they're full of anty-bodies.

Why does Tarzan shout so loudly?
Because it hurts when he pounds his chest.

What do you call two rhinos on a bicycle?
Optimistic.

Teacher: They say time flies like an arrow.
Pupil: Yes, but fruit flies like a banana.

What would you get if a python slipped into a tuba?
A snake in the brass.

What has 99 legs and one eye?
A pirate centipede.

What has three trunks, two tails, and six feet?
An elephant with spare parts.

Why couldn't the butterfly go to the dance?
Because it was a moth ball.

What did the boa constrictor say to his girlfriend?
"I have a crush on you!"

What do you get if you cross a parrot with a shark?
A bird that will talk your ear off.

What did the bee say when it returned to the hive?
"Honey, I'm home."

What happened to the cannibal lion?
He had to swallow his pride.

What should you do if a rhino charges you?
Pay him!

How did the rival apes settle their differences?
With a gorilla war.

What do you get if you cross an elephant with a parrot?
An animal that tells you everything it remembers.

What's black and white and red all over?
A zebra with a sunburn.

Why did the canary refuse to work in a coal mine?
He said it was beneath him.

What did the tiger say when he cut off his tail?
It won't be long now.

What's the medical term for memory loss in parrots?
Polynesia.

What line of work did the parrot take up after it swallowed a clock?
Politics.

Where do monkeys go to drink?
The monkey bars.

Why should you value an elephant's opinion?
Because it carries a lot of weight.

What do you call a snail on a turtle's shell?
A thrill seeker.

Why did the monkey take a banana to the doctor's?
Because it wasn't peeling well.

How do you start a firefly race?
By saying "On your marks, get set, glow!"

What do wasps do when they build a new nest?
They have a house-swarming party.

Knock, knock!
Who's there?
Cash!
Cash who?
**No thanks, but
I'd love a peanut!**

**Why did
Tarzan spend
so much time on
the golf course?**
He was perfecting
his swing.

What do you call a
failed lion tamer?
Claude Behind!

Why don't farmers grow bananas
any longer?
Because they're long enough already.

How does the vet check the tiger's teeth for cavities?
Very carefully!

How do you measure a cobra?
In inches, they don't have any feet.

First man: I took my son to the zoo last week.
Second man: Really? And which cage is he in now?

SiLLY SPELLS

**What happens when
a witch on a broomstick
brakes too hard?**
She flies off the handle.

How do witches tell the time?
With witch watches.

**Where does the wizards' school store its
weightlifting equipment?**
Behind the dumbbell door.

How do elves greet each other?
"Small world, isn't it?"

How do Jamaican ghosts style their hair?
In deadlocks!

SiLLY SPELLS

What happened to the witch who swallowed a poisonous toad?
She croaked!

What do you call a witch's garage?
A broom closet.

Who scared the troll under the bridge?
The billy ghosts Gruff.

Which jokes go down well with skeletons?
Rib ticklers!

Who said, "Get lost," to the Big Bad Wolf?
Little Rude Riding Hood.

SILLY SPELLS

What is a wizzerd?
A wizard who can't spell!

Knock, knock!
Who's there?
Al.
Al who?
Al huff and I'll puff and blow your house down!

What do you get if you cross a skeleton and a garden spade?
Skullduggery!

What kind of shoes do witches wear in the summer?
Open toad sandals!

Where do you find monster snails?
On the end of monsters' fingers!

SILLY SPELLS

What do you call
a fairy that has
never taken a
bath?
Stinkerbell!

What do you
get if you cross
a skeleton and
a dog?
An animal that buries itself!

Who's that at the door?
The invisible man.
Tell him I can't see him.

What did the headless ghost get when he fell through
a window?
A pane in the neck!

What do witches sing at Christmas?
Deck the Halls with Poison Ivy.

Why did the pixie move out of the toadstool?
Because there wasn't mushroom.

Why is Frankenstein's monster bad at school?
He doesn't have the brains he was born with!

Baby ogre: When I grow up, I want to drive a tank!
Mother ogre: Well, I certainly won't stand in your way!

How many guests has the zombie invited to his party?
It depends on who he could dig up!

What do monster children do on Halloween?
They go from door to door dressed as humans!

SILLY SPELLS

What's big, red, and eats rocks?
A big, red rock-eater!

What do ghostly police officers do?
They haunt down criminals!

Why don't giants speak to leprechauns?
They're no good at small talk.

Did you hear about the incredibly clever monster?
He was called Frank Einstein.

What do you call two witches who live together?
Broommates!

SILLY SPELLS

What do Italian ghosts eat for dinner?
Spookhetti!

What did the monster say to the scruffy werewolf?
"You look like you're going to the dogs!"

Why couldn't the wizard move?
He was spellbound!

Why was the skeleton's jacket in shreds?
Because he had very sharp shoulder blades!

Why would Snow White be a good judge?
Because she is the fairest in the land.

SiLLY SPELLS

Where do you normally find elves?
It depends where you left them!

Which fairy-tale creature has the most teeth?
A dragon?
No, the tooth fairy!

Why did the headless ghost go to the psychiatrist?
Because he wasn't all there!

What did the No Parking sign outside the witch's house say?
Violators will be toads!

How do two ghosts decide who owns something?
They fright each other for it!

SILLY SPELLS

What type of
spells did the
whirling wizard cast?
Dizzy spells.

What goes cackle,
squelch, cackle,
squelch?
A witch in soggy
tennis shoes.

What noise does a
witch's car make?
Broom, broom!

What do you call a vampire that hides in the kitchen?
Spatula!

What do you call a magician's assistant?
Magic Trixie!

SILLY SPELLS

Why didn't the witch sing a solo at the concert?
Because she had a frog in her throat.

Why was the ogre catching centipedes?
He wanted scrambled legs for breakfast!

Where would you find a suitable gift for a tortured ghost?
In a chain store!

What did the police do to the giant who ran away with
the circus?
They made him bring it back.

Which great detective is
three feet tall and has
pointed ears?
Sherlock Gnomes.

Did you hear about the vampire who fell asleep in the wrong coffin?
It was a grave mistake!

What happened to the boxer who got knocked out by Dracula?
He was out for the Count.

Knock, knock.
Who's there?
Aladdin.
Aladdin who?
Aladdin the street who wants to come in!

What is the difference between
a dragon and a mouse?
Have you had your eyes
tested recently?

SILLY SPELLS

Why can't you borrow money from a leprechaun?
Because he's always a little short.

Who lights up a haunted house?
The lights witch.

What did the big candle say to the little candle?
"I'm going out tonight."

Did you hear about the tiny, winged Egyptian king?
He was a fairy pharaoh!

How do you fix a jack-o'-lantern?
Use a pumpkin patch.

SILLY SPELLS

Why did the head druid keep falling over?
He couldn't get the staff.

What do you call a wizard who's really good at golf?
Harry Putter.

Why did the witch put her broom in the wash?
She wanted a clean sweep.

What do you call a warlock who tries to stop fights?
A peacelock.

SILLY SPELLS

Why are mermaids
easy to weigh?
Because they have
their own scales.

What does Medusa do
on a bad hair day?
She pays a visit to the
snake charmer.

Why was the giant's
hand only eleven
inches long?
An inch longer, and it
would be a foot.

What do you call a
female wizard?
Magic Wanda.

When do ghosts usually appear?
Just before somebody screams.

SILLY SPELLS

Why was Cinderella a terrible tennis player?
She kept running away from the ball.

How do you make a witch itch?
Take away the "w!"

When I grow up, I'd like to marry a ghost.
What would possess you to do that?

How did the Good Weather Wizard get his name?
He loved sunny spells.

How can you tell whether a leprechaun is enjoying himself?
He's Dublin over with laughter.

What parting gift was
the young werewolf
given when he left
home?
A comb!

What's the definition
of "deadline?"
A fence around a
graveyard!

Why do dragons sleep
all day?
So they can fight
knights!

What do you call a big, fat troll?
A wobblin' goblin.

What do you call a wizard
with a cold?
A blizzard.

SILLY SPELLS

Why do witches have painful joints?
They get broomatism.

Why did the ogre's mother knit him three socks as a birthday present?
Because he had grown another foot.

What does the witch use to keep her doors secure?
Warlocks!

What did the giant police officer eat for lunch?
Beef burglars!

Why did Jack Frost refuse to get married?
Because he got cold feet!

SiLLY SPELLS

Who grants your
wishes but smells
of fishes?
The fairy
cod-mother.

Why did the
dragon breathe
on the map of
the Earth?
Because he
wanted to set the world on fire.

What do you call a troll of average size?
Medi-ogre.

What happened to the man who didn't pay the exorcist's bill
on time?
He was repossessed.

What does a witch doctor ask his guests at the start of
a meal?
"Voodoo like to sit down?"

Which fairy-tale character has a black belt in kung fu?
The Ninja-bread Man.

What is a female elf called?
A shelf.

What is the first thing an ogre does when you give him a knife?
He writes out a chopping list!

What do you call a man who rescues drowning phantoms from the sea?
A ghost guard.

What happened to the witch with the gingerbread house?
She was eaten out of house and home!

HYSTERICAL HISTORY

When did early people start wearing uncreased clothes?
In the Iron Age!

What did Robin Hood wear to the Sherwood Forest ball?
A bow tie.

What was the moral of the story of Jonah and the whale?
You can't keep a good man down!

Teacher: Can you name a fierce warrior king?
Pupil: King Kong?

What sort of music did cavemen enjoy?
Rock music!

HYSTERICAL HISTORY

Teacher: Name an ancient musical instrument.
Pupil: An Anglo-saxophone?

What should you do if you see a caveman?
Go inside and explore, man!

What was Noah's job?
He was an ark-itect.

Why were undertakers in ancient Egypt such successful detectives?
They were good at wrapping up their cases.

What's purple and 5,000 miles long?
The grape wall of China.

HYSTERICAL HISTORY

Teacher: Surely you can remember what happened in 1776?
Pupil: It's all right for you, you were there!

Who was the fastest runner of all time?
Adam, because he was first in the human race!

Why did the king go to the dentist?
To get his teeth crowned.

Why did the student miss history class?
He had the wrong date.

Why was England so wet in the nineteenth century? Because Queen Victoria's reign lasted 64 years.

HYSTERICAL HISTORY

Which ancient leader invented seasonings?
Sultan Pepper!

Who succeeded the first
President of the United States?
The second one.

Why did the very first
fries not taste very
nice?
Because they
were fried in
ancient Greece!

Teacher: Can you
name a renowned
religious warrior?
Pupil: Attila the Nun!

Teacher: Where would you find a cowboy?
Pupil: In a field. And stop calling me "boy!"

What music do Egyptian mummies like best?
Wrap music!

HYSTERICAL HISTORY

What do you call the Roman Emperor who kept pet mice?
Julius Cheeser!

How did Moses cut the sea in half?
With a sea-saw.

Teacher: How did knights make chain mail?
Pupil: From steel wool?

Who built the Ark?
I have Noah idea.

Where were French traitors beheaded?
Just above the shoulders!

HYSTERICAL HISTORY

Two wrongs don't make a right, but what do two rights make?
The first plane!

Teacher: Why did Robin Hood steal from the rich?
Pupil: Because the poor didn't have anything worth stealing!

Teacher: How did the Dark Ages get their name?
Pupil: Because there were so many knights!

First Roman soldier: What's the time?
Second Roman soldier: XV past VIII.
First Roman soldier:
By the time I work
that out, it will
be midnight!

What is an archeologist?
Someone whose career is in ruins.

What do you call the king who invented the fireplace?
Alfred the Grate!

What did King Henry VIII do whenever he burped?
He issued a royal pardon.

Where was the Declaration of Independence signed?
At the bottom.

How did Vikings send secret messages?
By Norse code.

Which emperor should never have played with explosives?
Napoleon Blownapart!

Why do historians believe that Rome was built at night?
Because it wasn't built in a day.

In which battle was Alexander the Great killed?
His last one!

Where did Viking teachers send sick children?
To the school Norse.

What was King John's castle renowned for?
Its knight life.

Which historical character was always eating?
Attila the Hungry!

What did Robin Hood say when he was almost hit at the archery tournament?
"That was an arrow escape!"

Teacher: Today we're studying ancient Rome. Can anyone tell me what a forum was?
Pupil: A two-um plus a two-um?

What did Attila's wife say to get his attention?
"Over here, Hun."

What did the caveman give his girlfriend on Valentine's Day?
Ugs and kisses.

Why did King Arthur have a Round Table?
So that no one could corner him.

What do Alexander the Great and Billy the Kid have in common?
The same middle name.

How do we know that the ancient Romans had an expensive education?
Because they could all speak Latin.

Why couldn't the mummy answer the phone?
He was too wrapped up!

Who would referee a tennis match between Julius Caesar and Brutus?
A Roman umpire.

Who sailed on the ghost ship?
The skeleton crew.

Did prehistoric people hunt bear?
No, they wore clothes!

Why did the mammoth have a furry coat?
Because it would have looked silly in a parka.

What did Caesar say to Cleopatra?
Toga-ether we can rule the world!

What snack did the caveman like best?
A club sandwich.

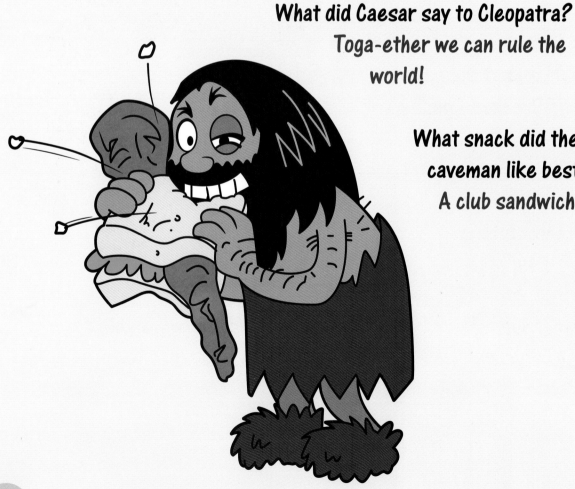

Which king had the largest crown?
The one with the biggest head!

Teacher: What came after the Stone Age and the Bronze Age?
Pupil: The sausage?

In which era did people sunbathe the most?
The Bronzed Age.

What did the ancient Egyptians call bad leaders?
Un-Pharaohs.

What happened to the knight who lost his left arm and left leg in battle?
He was all right in the end.

Where do Egyptian mummies go for a swim?
To the Dead Sea.

How did Columbus's men sleep on the boat?
With their eyes shut.

Why did Eve move to New York?
She fell for the Big Apple.

What do you call a blind dinosaur?
Doyouthinkhesaurus.

What has two eyes, two legs and two noses?
Two pirates!

HYSTERICAL HISTORY

Where did the pilgrims land when they came to America?
On their feet!

What did the executioner say to the former king?
It's time to head off!

What do you call a pyramid overlooking the Nile?
A tomb with a view.

What did the cowboy say when he saw a cow in a tree?
Howdy get there?

Which Egyptian pharaoh played the trumpet?
Tootin' Kamun.

HYSTERICAL HISTORY

What do history teachers talk about when they
get together?
The good old days.

What do you call a prehistoric monster when it is asleep?
A dino-snore.

Why did Columbus cross the ocean?
To get to the other tide.

Who made dinner for Robin Hood and his
Merry Men?
Frier Tuck.

Which knight designed King
Arthur's Round Table?
Sir Cumference!

HYSTERICAL HISTORY

What was the
first thing Queen
Elizabeth I did
when she
ascended the
throne?
She sat down.

Pupil: I wish I had
been born 1,000
years ago.
Teacher: Why is that?
Pupil: Because I wouldn't have
had to learn so much history!

How did the Roman cannibal feel about his
mother-in-law?
Gladiator.

What was the most popular movie in ancient Greece?
Troy Story.

What happened when the wheel was invented?
It caused a revolution.

Did Adam and Eve ever have a date?
No, but they had an apple!

Where was the Ink-an Empire?
In Pen-sylvania.

How was the Roman Empire cut in half?
With a pair of Caesars.

Where did Napoleon
keep his armies?
Up his sleevies.

Why did the court
jester swallow fire?
Because he wanted
to burn some
calories.

HYSTERICAL HISTORY

What happened when electricity was discovered?
Someone got a nasty shock.

Why did the nervous knight withdraw from the archery contest?
It was an arrowing experience.

How did Robin Hood tie his bootlaces?
With a long bow.

What did Thomas Edison's mother say when he showed her the electric light he had invented?
"That's wonderful, dear. Now turn it off and go to bed."

Why did the Romans build straight roads?
So the soldiers didn't go round the bend.

What did Mount Vesuvius say to Pompeii?
I lava you.

What do you call an archeologist who sleeps all the time?
Lazy bones.

Which protest by a group of cats and dogs took place in 1773?
The Boston Flea Party.

Why did Captain Cook sail to Australia?
It was too far to swim.

What did Columbus do after he crossed the Atlantic?
He dried his clothes.

Why did Cleopatra take milk baths? She couldn't find a cow tall enough for her to take a shower.

Which Viking explorer had a greenhouse on his longboat? Leaf Eriksson.

Why did the T. rex wear a bandage? He had a dino-sore!

What do you call George Washington's false teeth? Presi-dentures.

Which pirate told the most jokes? Captain Kidd.

Why did the pioneers cross America in covered wagons? Because they didn't want to wait 30 years for the first train.

Why was Charlemagne able to draw such straight lines?
He was a good ruler.

What did Noah use to find his way in the dark?
Floodlights.

What king invented fractions?
King Henry the $\frac{1}{8}$th.

Why were the first European settlers in America like ants?
Because they lived in colonies.

CRAZY COMPUTERS

CRAZY COMPUTERS

What do you call a flying printer?
An inkjet!

Spotted in the library:
How to Build a Shrink Ray by Minnie Mize

Where is the world's biggest computer?
In New York. It's the Big Apple!

What does a baby computer call its father?
Data!

Why did the medical computer go to prison?
It had performed an illegal operation.

CRAZY COMPUTERS

Where does the biggest spider in the universe live? On the World Wide Web.

What do you call a man with a speedometer in the middle of his forehead? Miles!

How do computers say goodbye?
"See you later, calculator!"

Teacher: Steven, what's a computer byte?
Pupil: I didn't even know they had teeth!

What do you get if you cross a computer with a lifeguard?
A screensaver.

CRAZY COMPUTERS

Why are birds always on the Internet?
They just love tweeting.

What was the robot doing at the gym?
Pumping iron.

Why did the robot boxer sit on the stove before the big match?
He wanted to strike while the iron was hot.

Which cookie do computers like best?
Chocolate microchip.

**If human babies are delivered by stork, how are
robot babies delivered?**
By crane!

CRAZY COMPUTERS

What did the computer nerd say when his mother opened
the curtains?
Wow, look at those graphics!

Why are evil robots so shiny?
Because there's no rust for the wicked.

Did you hear about the kid who had his ID stolen?
Now he's just a "k."

Spotted in the library:
Robots Are People Too by Anne Droid.

What happened to the robot
who put his shoes on the wrong feet?
He had to be rebooted.

CRAZY COMPUTERS

What's orange and points North?
A magnetic carrot.

First robot: Are you enjoying that book about magnetism?
Second robot: Yes, I can't put it down!

Why was the thirsty astronaut hanging out near the
computer keyboard?
He was looking for the space bar.

Did you hear about the couple who adopted a calculator?
It made a great addition to the family.

Why did the Apple
Mac programmer
live in
the dark?
Because he
refused to
use Windows.

Why did the boy bring a surfboard to school?
The teacher said they were going to be surfing the Internet.

Why was the computer such a terrific golfer?
It had a hard drive.

How do lumberjacks get on the Internet?
They log on.

What do you call a man with a cable coming out of his ear?
Mike!

What do you buy for someone who already has all the latest gadgets?
A burglar alarm.

Why did the robot get angry?
Someone kept pushing his buttons!

What do you get if you cross a large computer and a hamburger?
A Big Mac!

Why do robots never feel queasy?
They have cast iron stomachs.

Why did the pupil fall asleep in computer class?
He was feeling key-bored.

What do you give a robot who feels like a light snack?
Some 60-watt bulbs!

What's the difference between computer hardware and software?
Hardware is the stuff that you can kick when it doesn't work.

What goes in one year and out the other?
A time machine!

Teacher: Give me an example of cutting-edge technology.
Pupil: A pair of scissors?

My computer
is powered by
clockwork.
Really?
No, I was just winding
you up.

What music do
robots like to
listen to?
Heavy metal!

CRAZY COMPUTERS

How can you tell if a robot is happy to see you?
Because his eyes light up.

What do you get from robot sheep?
Steel wool.

Why did the computer programmer give up his job?
He lost his drive.

Why was the electrified robot so badly behaved?
It didn't know how to conduct itself.

Did you hear about the robot dog?
His megabark was worse than his megabyte.

What do you call a robot who turns into a tractor?
A trans-farmer!

Where do cool
mice live?
In mouse pads.

Did you know that
my computer can do
the gardening?
Can it really?
Yes, it's made
with cutting-hedge
technology.

Which city has no people?
Electricity.

Did you hear about the two TVs who got married?
Their reception was excellent.

CRAZY COMPUTERS

Why did the boy and girl robots call things off after their first date?
There was no spark.

Why did the robot kiss his girlfriend?
He just couldn't resistor.

How did the inventor of the jetpack feel?
He was on cloud nine!

Why did the storekeeper refuse to serve italic fonts?
He didn't like their type.

Where did the tightrope walker meet his girlfriend?
Online.

CRAZY COMPUTERS

How do snowmen get online?
They use the Winternet.

How does a tiny robot say goodbye?
With a micro-wave.

Brad: Have you seen my high-tech watch belt?
Suzie: It sounds like a waist of time.

Why did the witch buy a computer?
She needed a spell-checker!

What do
astronauts
eat out of?
Satellite
dishes.

CRAZY COMPUTERS

How many ears does a robot have?
Three: a left ear, a right ear, and just in case they go wrong, an engine-ear.

What was wrong with the robot shepherd?
He didn't have enough RAM.

What do you call a man with a car on his head?
Jack!

Why was the boy happy when he hurt his eye?
Because the doctor gave him an iPad.

Why did the inventor stuff herbs in the disk drive of his computer?
He was trying to build a thyme machine.

CRAZY COMPUTERS

Why couldn't the computer take off its hat?
Because the caps lock was on.

Spotted in the library:
How to Fix Just About Anything by Andy Mann.

Teacher: Look at the state of the classroom computer. I want that screen cleaned so well I can see my own face in it!
Pupil: But then it will crack!

What do you call a short band leader?
A semi-conductor.

Why did the computer catch a cold?
Someone kept leaving its Windows open.

CRAZY COMPUTERS

How did the inventor of the space rocket feel?
Over the moon!

What do you call a robot standing in the rain?
Rusty!

What invention is sillier than glow-in-the-dark sunglasses for midnight sunbathing?
Underwater umbrellas for scuba divers!

Why did the silly girl put her letters in the microwave?
She wanted to use Hotmail.

Why did they have to call off the computer race?
The competitors kept crashing.

CRAZY COMPUTERS

Who won the Oscar for best android actor?
Robot Downey, Jr.

How did the scientist invent insect repellent?
He started from scratch.

There's never anything on TV, is there?
I don't know about that, there's a vase on top of ours.

Have you been on the optician's website?
It's a site for sore eyes.

Why did the computer programmer give up his life of crime?
He couldn't hack it any more.

What do you call a nervous robot?
A shy-borg.

How do lazy spiders decorate their homes?
They hire web designers.

Do you think scientists will ever invent flying desserts?
No, that's pie in the sky.

What happened when the bossy android charged for too long?
It went on a power trip!

How did the lazy office worker get his daily exercise?
He turned on his computer and clicked on "run."

Teacher: Why have you stopped typing?
Pupil: It was making me feel keyed up.

Did you hear about the computer programmer whose illegal activities made him sick?
He gave himself a hacking cough.

Did you have any success with Internet dating?
Yes, it was love at first site.

Why didn't two computers get along?
They got their wires crossed.

What do you call an android with oars?
A row-bot.

What did one calculator say to the other calculator? You can count on me.

What do robot office workers eat?
A staple diet.

Why did the girl mouse decide not to ask the boy mouse on a second date?
They just didn't click.

Computer repair man: What's wrong with this laptop, sir?
Customer: Thespacebarseemstobestuck.

Have you heard about the new online service for short-sighted people?
It's called the Squinternet.

FUN ON THE FARM

FUN ON THE FARM

How do chicks get out of their shells?
They look for the eggs-it.

What's brown and sticky?
A stick!

What do you get if you cross a sheepdog and a fruit?
A melon-collie!

How do you make a chicken stew?
Keep it waiting for a couple of hours.

What do you get when you cross a rooster with a duck?
A bird that gets up at the quack of dawn.

Which ballet do pigs
like best?
Swine Lake.

Teacher: How would
you hire a farm worker?
Pupil: Put a brick under
each leg.

What did the pig say when the
farmer grabbed him by the tail?
"That's the end of me."

Knock, knock!
Who's there?
Farmer.
Farmer who?
Farmer distance, your house looks much bigger!

What happened when the sheep pen broke?
The sheep had to use a pencil.

FUN ON THE FARM

What's green and sings in the vegetable patch?
Elvis Parsley.

Knock, knock!
Who's there?
Lettuce.
Lettuce who?
Lettuce in and you'll find out!

What did the horse say when it fell over?
"I've fallen and I can't giddy-up."

What do horses tell their children at bedtime?
Pony tales!

Patient: Doctor, what can I do to help me get to sleep?
Doctor: Have you tried counting sheep?
Patient: Yes, but then I have to wake up to drive home again!

FUN ON THE FARM

What do you give a sick pig?
Oinkment!

How did the musical farmer know which note to sing?
He used a pitchfork!

Why should you be careful where you step when it rains cats and dogs?
You could step in a poodle!

What do you call the wages paid to a gardener?
His celery!

What do you call a sleeping bull?
A bulldozer.

What do you get if you cross a chicken with a kangaroo?
Pouched eggs!

How did the pig with laryngitis feel?
Dis-gruntled.

Why do roosters curse all the time?
They are fowl-mouthed.

What did the waiter say when the horse walked into the café?
Why the long face?

What did the chicken say when it laid a square egg?
Owwww!

What did the flamenco-dancing farmer say to his chickens?
"Oh, lay!"

Why did the rubber chicken cross the road?
She wanted to stretch her legs.

What do you get if you feed gunpowder to a chicken?
An egg-splosion!

Where do horses stay in hotels?
The bridle suite.

What did the farmer use to paint the new sty?
Pigment.

What do you call a factual TV show about sheep?
A flock-umentary!

Why did the goose cross the road?
To prove she wasn't chicken!

Patient: Doctor, I got trampled by a load of cows!
Doctor: So I herd!

What do you give a pony with a cold?
Cough stirrup!

Why should you never tell your secrets to a piglet?
Because they might squeal!

How do alien farmers round up their sheep?
They use tractor beams!

What do you get when you cross a chicken and a fox?
Just the fox.

How can you cook turkey that really tickles the
taste buds?
Leave the feathers on!

How many pigs do you
need to make a smell?
A phew!

What do you call
a cow with an
out-of-date map?
Udderly lost!

Where do cows go for history lessons?
To a mooseum!

Which fairy tale do pigs like best?
Slopping Beauty.

If a small duck is called a duckling, what do you call
a small pen?
An inkling!

Mother: You can't keep a pig in your bedroom, what about the terrible smell?
Child: Don't worry, he'll soon get used to it!

What do you get if you cross a donkey and Christmas?
Muletide greetings!

FUN ON THE FARM

What do you call a dog with a bunch of roses?
A collie-flower!

Why did the farmer's dog keep chasing his tail?
He was trying to make ends meet.

How does a sheep finish a letter?
Sincerely ewes.

Why did the chicken cross the playground?
To get to the other slide!

What sort of jokes do chickens like best?
Corny ones!

What do you get if you cross a cow and a jogging machine?
A milk shake!

Is chicken soup good for your health?
Not if you're the chicken!

What grows down as it grows up?
A goose!

Why is that farmer setting fire to the plants in his field?
He's growing baked beans!

What do you call a man who keeps rabbits?
Warren!

FUN ON THE FARM

What says, "Moo, baa, woof, quack, meow, oink?"
A sheep that speaks foreign languages!

What do you get if you cross a cow with a camel?
Lumpy milkshakes!

Where do sheep get shorn?
At the baa-baas!

What has lots of ears, but can't hear anything at all?
A cornfield.

How does your dog get into the house?
Through the labra-door!

FUN ON THE FARM

What does it mean if you find a set of horse shoes?
A horse is walking around in his socks!

Why did the boy stand behind the horse?
He thought he might get a kick out of it.

What do you get from a forgetful cow?
Milk of amnesia.

What did the alien say to the plant?
"Take me to your weeder!"

If you had fifteen cows and five goats, what would you have?
Plenty of milk!

Patient: Doctor, I feel like a goat!
Doctor: Really? And how are the kids?

Why did the lamb call the police?
It had been fleeced!

What do you get from a pampered cow?
Milk that's spoiled.

What do you call a
pig with three eyes?
A piiig.

Why did the
chicken run out
on to the basketball
court?
Because the referee
whistled for a fowl!

Young man, can you reach that package of beef from the top of the freezer?
No ma'am. The steaks are too high.

What do cows eat for breakfast?
Moosli!

What did the polite sheep say to his friend at the gate?
After ewe.

Have sheep ever flown?
No, but swine flu.

What did the duck say when she bought lipstick?
Put it on my bill!

Why did the two pigs go to Las Vegas for their vacation?
To play on the slop machines.

How did the farmer find his lost sheep?
He tractor down.

What do you call a cow with only his two left legs?
Lean beef.

When do you know it's time for a farmer's family to go to sleep?
When it's pasture bedtime.

What has five fingers and drives a tractor?
A farm hand.

What kind of animal goes OOM?
A cow walking backward!

What do you call a tale with a twist at the end?
A pigtail!

Why did the farmer think someone was spying on him?
There were moles all over his field.

A cross between a cocker spaniel and a poodle is a called a cockapoo. So what do you call a cross between a cockapoo and a poodle?
A cock-a-poodle-do!

What do you call a chicken crossing the road?
Poultry in motion.

How do hens dance?
Chick to chick!

What is the best way
to carve wood?
Whittle by whittle.

Why did the farmer
drive a steamroller over
his field?
He wanted to grow
mashed potatoes.

Why do male deer
need braces?
Because they have
buck teeth.

Why did the rooster get a tattoo?
He wanted to impress the chicks.

What do you get from an invisible cow?
Evaporated milk.

First cow in a field: Moo.
Second cow: Ohhh, I was going to say that!

Why did the ram run over the cliff?
He didn't see the ewe turn!

What was the result when two silkworms had a race?
It ended in a tie.

Teacher: Who can tell me which sea creature eats its prey two at a time?
Pupil: Noah's shark!

What do sea captains tell their children at night?
Ferry tales.

Where do fish sleep?
On a waterbed!

Teacher: What musical instrument do Spanish fishermen play?
Cast-a-nets!

Why don't clams give to charity?
Because they're shellfish.

PLEASE GIVE GENEROUSLY

Teacher: Why was no one able to play cards on Noah's Ark?
Pupil: Because Noah stood on the deck!

What kind of noise makes an oyster grouchy?
A noisy noise annoys an oyster!

Teacher: Where do you find starfish?
Pupil: In the Galack Sea!

Where can you find an ocean with no water?
On a map.

Which beach item gets wetter the more it dries?
A towel.

What lies at the bottom of the ocean and shakes?
A nervous wreck.

Customer: Waiter, what's wrong with this fish?
Waiter: Long time, no sea.

What happened when the restless sleeper bought himself a waterbed?
He got seasick.

Lifeguard: You can't fish on this stretch of beach!
Boy with fishing rod: I'm not, I'm teaching my pet worm to swim.

What happened when the salmon went to Hollywood?
He became a starfish.

Why don't fish parents tell their children about electric eels?
They're just too shocking.

What music do they play in underwater nightclubs?
Sole music!

What did the passing seagull say to the pilot of the motorboat with no engine?
"How's it going?"

Which game is popular with fish?
Name That Tuna.

Which two fish can you wear on your feet?
A sole and an eel.

Did you hear about the two fish in a tank?
One was driving, and the other was manning the guns.

Wife: Doctor, is there any hope for my husband? He thinks he's a shipwreck.
Doctor: I'm afraid he's sunk, ma'am.

Why did the man go swimming in his best clothes?
He thought he needed a wet suit.

How do jellyfish police capture criminals?
In sting operations.

What did the walrus do after he read the sad book?
He started to blubber.

Watership Down

How can you tell that the ocean is feeling friendly?
It keeps waving at you.

Which fish once ruled Russia?
The tsar-dine.

How can you tell two octopuses are dating?
Because they walk along arm in arm in arm in arm in arm in arm in arm in arm!

What can you expect from a clever crab?
Snappy answers!

How could you give yourself an injury gathering shellfish?
You might pull a mussel.

How do fish go into business?
They start on a small scale.

What day do fish hate?
Fry day.

Where do ocean scientists keep their coffee mugs?
On the continental shelf.

Where do fish keep their savings?
In the river bank!

What do you call a man floating up and down on the sea?
Bob.

What happened when the boat carrying red paint crashed into one carrying blue paint?
Both crews were marooned.

Who stole the soap from the bathtub?
A robber duckie.

Why are dolphins
smarter than humans?
Because they can
train humans to
stand by the side
of the pool and
throw them fish.

What is the
traditional anthem of
the pig navy?
"Oinkers Aweigh."

Why didn't the sea captain's radio work in rough seas?
It was on the wrong wavelength.

What kind of fish are useful in cold weather?
Skates.

OUT TO SEA

What do sea monsters eat?
Fish and ships!

What's fluffy and green?
A seasick poodle.

Why did the crab cross the road?
To get to the other tide.

Where is the safest place to see
a man-eating fish?
In a seafood restaurant.

What grades did
the pirate get in
school?
High seas.

OUT TO SEA

Which salad ingredient is the most dangerous for ocean liners?
Iceberg lettuce.

Who held the baby octopus for ransom?
Squidnappers!

What's the best medicine for seasickness?
Vitamin sea.

What do you get if you cross a bad golfer and an outboard motor?
I'm not sure, but I bet it goes, "Putt, putt, putt, putt."

Which fish come out at night?
Starfish.

Who wins all the money at the undersea poker games?
Card sharks.

What happens if you cross an electric eel with a sponge?
You get a shock absorber.

Why do pirates have a hard time learning the alphabet?
Because they spend so long at "C."

Why do whales sing?
Because they can't talk!

How do you close an envelope underwater?
With a seal.

OUT TO SEA

What runs and runs without ever getting out of breath?
A river.

What do the underwater police travel in?
Squid cars!

What sort of snacks can you buy on a Chinese boat?
Junk food!

How did Robinson Crusoe survive after his ship sank?
He found some soap and washed himself ashore.

Why wouldn't the sailor eat any fruitcake?
He was worried about dangerous currants.

OUT TO SEA

What sort of boats do clever schoolchildren travel on?
Scholar-ships!

Which vegetables do pirates like best?
Aaaaartichokes.

What did the deep-sea diver yell when he got caught in seaweed?
"Kelp!"

What do you get if you meet a shark in the Arctic Ocean?
Frostbite.

What did Cinderella wear when she went diving?
Glass flippers.

Which sea creature can also fly?
A pilot whale.

What do you call a gull that flies over a bay?
A bay-gull.

Why are goldfish orange?
The water makes them rusty.

Why did the surfer wear a baseball glove?
Because he wanted to catch a wave.

What do you call a delinquent octopus?
A crazy, mixed-up squid!

What is in the middle of a jellyfish?
A jellybutton.

How do you keep in touch with a fish?
You drop it a line.

What do whales like to chew?
Blubber gum.

How do fish get to school?
By octobus.

Why did the burglar buy a surfboard?
He wanted to start a crime wave!

Who is the
ocean's most
dangerous outlaw?
Billy the Squid.

Where do mermaids go to see movies?
The dive-in.

What did the fisherman say to the magician?
"Pick a cod, any cod."

How much sand would be in a hole the size of a house?
None. Holes are empty!

Why did Captain Hook cross the road?
To get to the second-hand store.

What do you get when you cross a bee with a seagull?
A beagle.

How does a penguin feel when it is left all alone?
Ice-olated.

What can you put into a barrel full of water to make it lighter?
A hole.

What is the coldest animal in the sea?
The blue whale.

Why do sea lions
swim in salt water?
Because pepper
makes them
sneeze.

Which fish go
to heaven when
they die?
Angelfish.

Why did the
ship's captain
look fed up?
He had a sinking feeling.

Why don't traffic lights ever
go swimming?
They take too long to change.

I'm on a seafood diet.
Are you losing weight?
No, because every time I see food, I eat it.

How did the dolphin make decisions?
It would flipper coin.

Who is the
head of the
underwater
Mafia?
The codfather.

What kind of
fish likes to eat
between meals?
A snackerel.

What game do fish
like to play at parties?
Tide and seek.

What did the pirate say to the woman in the shoe store?
"Where's my booties?"

What fish do knights like best?
Swordfish.

How does a boat show affection?
It hugs the shore.

How do lighthouse keepers communicate with each other?
With shine language.

What can fly underwater?
A mosquito in a submarine.

What do you use to cut the ocean in half?
A seasaw.

Which fish are the best at home-improvement projects?
Hammerhead sharks.

Which fish works in a hospital?
A plastic sturgeon.

What happens to a green rock when you throw it into the Red Sea?
It gets wet.

What do you call a baby squid?
A little squirt.

Which sea creatures are the biggest cry babies?
Whales.

What's the best way to stuff a lobster?
Take it out for pizza and ice cream.